TRUE NORTH

The Ernest Sandeen Prize in Poetry

EDITOR
John Matthias

1997, *True North*, Stephanie Strickland

TRUE
NORTH

Stephanie Strickland

University of Notre Dame Press
Notre Dame, Indiana

Library of Congress Cataloging-in-Publication Data
Strickland, Stephanie.
    True North / Stephanie Strickland.
        p.   cm. — (Ernest Sandeen prize in poetry)
    ISBN 0-268-01899-5 (alk. paper)
    I. Title.   II. Series.
PS3569.T69543T78   1996   96-27136
811′.54—dc20   CIP

Grateful acknowledgment is made to the following publications in which these poems, or earlier versions of them, first appeared: *American Letters & Commentary* for "Preservation of Order"; *The American Voice* for "*Jus Suum*: What Can Never Be Taken"; *The Bellingham Review* for "Linguisticuffs"; *Big Allis* for "Numbers Nesting . . . 1" as "1 Natural Numbers" and "Numbers Nesting . . . 5" as "5 (Imaginary Numbers)"; *DoubleTake* for "Pregnancy"; *The Kenyon Review* for "Striving All My Life," "The Lover Wishes to Be of Unending . . ." ("True North 1"), "Our Home the Earth" ("True North 2"), "It's Hard" ("True North 3"), "Strategem Strategem" as "Strategem—Strategem" ("True North 4"), "It's Easy" ("True North 5"), and "Young Willard Gibbs Is a Physicist"; *New Virginia Review* for "Guidance," "Narrowness of Narrow Path Endured," and "Who"; *Notre Dame Review* for "Casting of Bells Gives Way to Casting of Cannon" and "Even Purits Forced to Re-cog"; *The Paris Review* for "A History of Bearing Greek Gifts" and "Iris an Illusion"; *Pig Iron: The Epistolary Form & the Letter as Artifact* for "Time-Capsule Contents"; *Poet Lore* for "American Speech" as "American Speech 1," "It Is You Talking Just as Much . . ." as "American Speech 2," "Articulate Among Us" as "American Speech 3," "From Plain to Pure" as "American Speech 4," and "American Artificers" as "American Speech 5"; *Prairie Schooner* for "Heaven and Earth, 1666," "On First Looking into . . ." as "Diringer's *The Alphabet: A Key to the History of Mankind*," "Real Toads," and "The Romans Captured Archimedes"; *State Street Reader* for "Real Life Is White in Connecticut"; *Synaesthetic* for "A Frequent Dream . . . Tremendously Widened" as "A Frequent Dream"; *Tinfish* for "Lodged in a Nursery Glass"; and *West Branch* for "Prometheus, or The Eagle's Prey" as "Prometheus." I wish to express thanks to Yaddo, the MacDowell Colony, the Ragdale Foundation, the National Endowment for the Arts, and the National Endowment for the Humanities for awards that supported this work.

Contents

The children . . . were born with knives in their brains. . . .

> —Ralph Waldo Emerson, as quoted by
> Harriet H. Robinson, mill girl, *Loom & Spindle*

And do you think the words of your book are certainly true? "Yea, verily."

> —John Bunyan, *The Pilgrim's Progress*

*Herman has taken to writing poetry. You need not tell anyone,
for you know how such things get around.*

> —Mrs. Melville, in a letter to her mother

TRUE NORTH

The Mother-Lost World

On First Looking into Diringer's The Alphabet: A Key
to the History of Mankind

I wanted . . . a *Guneaform*—a woman's form—of writing
and thought, perhaps, Cuneiform it, so tactile that script, palpable
wedges pressed in wet clay: writing "at once," as a fresco

is painted. But in this book, in the pictographs
that underlie Cuneiform, there is only one sign for woman,
pudendum. Slavegirl and male servant, also

given by genital description.
Man is head, with mouth in it, plus beard.
I thought apart from Diringer's claim, *origin* of alphabets,

this script is just one instance. Hieroglyphic
determinatives for man and woman in Egypt look more
matched, both stickfigure-like, both kneeling on one shin— Except

the woman has longer hair, no arms, no *difference* between
first- and second-person-singular. How quietly here ancient grammar states
what our marital law, or canon teaching on abortion, legislates:

"I am—not only yours—but you."
I began to wonder whether, somewhere in the world, different
thinking existed. Flipping through the book,

I was struck by Chinese trigrams, their elegant
abstraction: just three lines
above each other meant, the footnote said, sky and dry and prime

and creative: grandfather-life. Slashed, into six
little lines, the sign meant secondarily
and destruction, and foreboding, and grandmother, and earth.

Later Chinese for man, an upright stroke, hook rising to the left.
For woman, a buckling crook, large bundle at the shoulder.
Woman, next to woman, meaning quarrel—

and man, next to word, meaning *true.*
I did find toward the end one group of people, the Yao
or Miao, or Miao-tzu tribe, called

by the Chinese "wild Southern barbarians."
Fifty thousand in Vietnam and Laos before our war.
The Yao had, I found nowhere else, four

different signs of *equal* complication:
mother, father, person, heart
—but as I said, wiped out.

Who Counts, Counts

Baby and you
—and me,
we will make three,

      but baby-and-me
      are different: we're two-
      who-are-one.

So, together, five—or we *were*, when
I-was-two-in-one,
but

      wishing, it was so hot
      that summer, I was wishing
      we were two.

You and me, we've been two
who were one as well, but nobody thinks
that's the same, or

      a problem. How
      many of us were there *really*,
      when

I-was-two-who-were-one? Was it
five: us-two + we-three?
Or three?

      Or two.
      You said, "If it came
      —God forbid—to that, well then,

just
two." You meant, should it come,
Godsent, to some crux,

      should push
      come to knife,
      just

Baby and you.

A History of Bearing Greek Gifts

FOR BRISEIS[+]

She so overestimates her strength, she plans to come back
from the Camp unscathed—unscathed from rape.
In fact, she is crazed: alone in the fog;

embrace, as she will, she cannot warm
the sword beside him. Needs fur, eiderdown. Found
in bed, aborted. In blood. Beside her,

the bones—and lassitude—of an infant
she can't think how to feed, can't remember
to feed, enough, but then,

who *can*
give these gifts back: Greek horses—Greek hatred
for strangers? For daughters. Tending

a seashell—not hungry herself,
or so she imagines—to tendrils of vine
she croons, *Though we suck*

now, on this gruel
of seafoam and sunlight, it won't always be
so. We're going to

be Animal, I tongue-tip,
I nipple—you,
fontanel.

[+] ". . . I shall take the fair-cheeked Briseis, / your prize, I myself going to your shelter, that you may learn well / how much greater I am than you, and another man may shrink back / from likening himself to me. . . ."—Agamemnon to Achilles, *Iliad* I, 184–87.

Preservation of Order

Encoded
at the source and handed down, order never
gets better, it gets distorted.

A new kind of Spiraling order arrives
on earth with backbone—*Dr. William Carlos Williams, the poet*
and obstetrician, said a poem is

a spine trying to go on without breaking down into chaos
or cliché—a new Scribe comes into play, a new Script (self-written)
to preserve what *is*, even as it does re-score itself: Mammalian DNA, 1%

pragmatic, 99% a game-arcade of Rule & Form. As the eggborn
are replaced by the placentals, by intimate fluid
identity, by seep
                    —*Williams really said*
a poem is beleaguered, a line of understanding that is
always breaking down—
                              the egg is replaced
by a parasitic cannibal, the fetal
creature living

on
the mother
body.

For 70 million years
so far, the mother's body, her self-monitor
immunity, tricked: accepting
                              the intimate suppliant
as passenger, not enemy; not self either, not meant to be
absorbed—*Dr. Williams said: "The goal*
                              of writing
is to keep a beleaguered line of understanding which has movement
from breaking down and becoming a hole into which we sink. . . ." No

baby its own—immune—system until after it is born, until some time after.
But the mother knows, she knew, it *is* another person. As God in Eden,
when word came to Him, *Let Us make Man*, knew,

before Creation. This is not a Mystery—this is like a poem
I have yet to write, and in which I will let the line
become a hole. The mystery is how

what is rooted in being known
about (disappears) as
it's created.

Lodged in a Nursery Glass

Embryo, instar,
      fatal creature,

nestling
      there, precursor and pre-
figurer:

      no trope.
A more expensive bargain
      pact: a patented genomic sac,

and stainless act, for unto us an infant
      TechnI.con,™ in fact,

is born:
      a real being, being re-
hearsed for the real

      [per-]Son
to come.

Pregnancy

I wish I knew
them better, those infant
explorers;

I wish I knew more
of them, single cells in the primitive
streak: how they know when—each one free-

moving—to go away; how they
know, one by one, to slip their mooring, to become
a sex cord, a neural arch, the heart. I wish I could see

the heart's rudiment
form, see mantle edges thicken into a tube: the heart,
a hole, a closed pocket

inside. I feel
undulations that take hours, even
days, squeezing one way, or the other. No one

understands it, not by law,
not by science,
what this layered movement

is, how
it knows
what it's doing, where to go,

when to stop.

Figures of Speech

Tropes pertain to their instance. They give an appearance
of tropical wealth, because description befits
the simple, where with something complex

description is beggared, description retreats, re-levels
itself as a Law only three or four pencil marks
are required for: the marks like seeds, that full

of unreelable display. To describe much more
than a simple instance, you must say
much less, and finally point, because complexity *is*

its own best—shortest—description. Jonathan
Edwards: "We have so far lost respect for God
that we are openly permitting benevolent writers the liberty

of fabricating out of nature whatever meanings
exhibit . . . ingenuity. The Sun can stand for anything,
Resurrection, approbation of George I, harvest, success. . . ."

The Lover Wishes to Be of Unending

secret service to the beloved. When the beloved is God,
this is hard—
except for the atheist.

A magnetic compass,
even without interference from nearby
masses of iron—the steel frame of a building—doesn't point

to the North Pole; it points
somewhere
in Hudson's Bay.

To find, or to reckon
the direction true North, you need to get help
from the spinning earth.

A lover who eschews force—*anyone*
coming forward to speak
is using force—

can only
stand waiting, here
on earth, where

there *are* no
straight
lines.

Blue Planet Blues

Guidance

Guardian
ring of light: flashing heart
of our system to orient, truly— By speed,

a trial time: two racing beams
streak past each other on a tight turn, *lean,*
and one of them

homes faster: clockwork
governs laser gyroscopes, but don't stop
here. Go beyond light technology:

a hollowed sphere
of beryllium, suspended in
a magnetic cradle

nothing touches,
even air. Hush. All we know
of how to orient

is here, the human mind
and finger, stretched.
Where have we laid

our cradle?
In the Trident,
the MX.

Time-Capsule Contents

1 Sermon: *What Will Be Left?*

Weather, certainly. Even
the ticking earth must thaw. Genetic law

will prove to be present, each still-born defect
confirmation. Murmurous

why-lords, why this generation? This destruction
of our marrow. More than all

these, memory of Promise, her chrysalis
jeans, her eyes extraordinarily

bright, shadowed with
mascara: Honey,

as she was,
in heat, in bloom, in slow

motion, left, locked
in the projector.

2 Transcription of Outtakes from Pre-trial Deposition

I don't think flu
should be our *whole* answer.
Let's go over it, again.

Be more specific, if you can.
This record has to hold
up, for generations. We do know,

Colonel, you've been ill.
And you say, you were misled,
or did you say, unnerved,

by a woman selling apples
who tried to stop you
on your way to work.

You ordered, ***Two*** *if by land*,
you chose, ***North*** *Dakota*,
you swore, *If your* ***right*** *hand*

offend you— Is this
the statement, Sir, you wish
to give the court?

3 Journal Entry

In the shelter, I doze.
I remember
Indian October. An aquarium of birchleaves

flowing around us
slowly,
like nectar. Home loaves.

Dark oven. Syrup
on our fingers. Chrysanthemums
heavy, in the sugarbowl

of summer.

Linguisticuffs

I think I doubt the existence of an ideal,
explicit sentence at the core

of each one offered. Wouldn't
the core (like a rainbow) disappear

as you come closer into clouds
of structure on a level *other*

than the one you first
perceived?

No inherent
end: no pot of gold—

you die, you lose "interest," but the trail
remains. Now for a *theory*

of language, what can
be said is more important than

what is,
but not to us: we are

surpassingly interested
in the actual

message, chosen
and sent.

"A summer job in Waterbury, Connecticut, with the American Brass Company turned into a permanent one. . . .

"I still have vivid sensual memories of that time: The smell of burning lard oil. Streams of molten brass in the casting shop. Some of the last coke-fired pit furnaces in operation, and men drawing crucibles, skimming and pouring the metal. The magnificent row of rolling mills, all driven continuously by a Corliss engine with a huge flywheel and a shaft running the full length of the large shop. The dance and clangor of drop and screw presses; and a sympathetic feeling for the pressure in the extrusion presses. Men seizing red-hot snakes of copper, threading them curving back and forth through the wire rod mill at Ansonia. (To this day a frequent dream is of wandering through complex assemblies of industrial buildings full of such machines, in search of something I never find.)

". . . unlike the academic, who thinks his ideas seven days a week, as an industrial employee I had weekends free, and these enabled me to exploit the Sterling Library at nearby Yale University and develop my historical interests.

"World War II ended all this. . . . I went to Los Alamos to direct the work on metallurgy. This involved preparing the fissionable metal for the cores of the Hiroshima and Nagasaki bombs. . . .

"The work was applied science at its best. . . . The physical environment of mountains, mesa, and forest provided an inspiring backdrop. . . . It was a very different world from the Connecticut industrial town, and my intellectual horizons were tremendously widened as I found myself able to play a part in association with many of the greatest physicists of the time.

"Not only in the laboratory—I frequently went hiking in the mountains with Bethe, Fermi, Weisskopf, Teller, G.I. Taylor, and once even cajoled Johnny von Neumann into a short scramble up the Quemazon trail. . . . All this served to intensify the intellectual slant of my mind that had been barely perceptible before, and it made the appeal of the intellectual world irresistible."

—Cyril Stanley Smith, *A Search For Structure,*
Cambridge, MA: MIT Press, 1981.

Casting of Bells Gives Way to Casting of Cannon

Poles of knowing: Bell and Endor; one, a *theorem*,
one, a Witch[+] of.

Saul and Macbeth, who both seek power beyond
what's possible, seek it through knowledge—a cult knowledge

retained in one Weird woman (after the countryside has been cleared
of women, who fly, who flew, who chatter

like wrens). What does the Witch teach? Only
what is: "Saul," she says, "give it up."

(But bred, punished, conditioned
into caution about home truth, how did she dare

to speak? All her sisters,
"cut off.") Bell's

theorem?[++] The same. A frame for constraining. To the king's
desire, *Look into seeds of time and say which grows, which*

not, it says no
way is there to go a way not gone, no way to grow

(prognosticate) unchosen seed (untaken
paths), no going back on dice once cast, no *might-*

have-been that hangs around unless
it was: no *could*

but *is.* Poles set
a bound. Now, King (S(aul)/M(ac)),

they say, *Behold,*
Time rides, but time comes. . . .

[+] 1 Samuel 28.7–9: "Then said Saul unto his servants, Seek me a woman that hath
a familiar spirit, that I may go to her, and enquire of her. . . . And Saul disguised himself,
and put on other raiment, and he went, and two men with him, and they came to the
woman [the Witch of Endor] by night. . . . And the woman said unto him, Behold, thou
knowest what Saul hath done, how he hath cut off those that have familiar spirits, and
the wizards, out of the land: wherefore then layest thou a snare for my life, to cause me
to die?"

[++] J. S. Bell, *Physics* 1, 195 (1964).

The Whole

—it means force is deformation,

it means

what is assumed

fundamental

is derived: it means a point is a collection—reform-
ulating physics—a collection of twistors (there) at that point: all possible
lightpaths. Maybe all

calculation

should use complex numbers.
Maybe

the real world we see
is a real projection of something
—complex: the solid

part of a table, *one part,* each quadrillion. And between these
bullets?

Nothing

is less certain. The party of the hard part, the a-for-apple
real part, halts and stops us: where and when;
but the b-for-broom sweeps

through in flashing angular directions,
set spinning as it swings—and
going somewhere:

homing to the pole
of its Polar-i-
za-tion.

Presto! How the Universe Is Made

On your Mark, one first O/riginal Form; *Get set,* a second
angular Segment; *Go*—the next step, a Rule replacing
each straight side in the first by the second; if I take

a box and for each side of that box substitute a cone
or peak, to make a kind of star—then do *again*
what I did before: take the star-box

and where I find a straight-line replace it
with a peak, to make a *starrier* star, nesting the shape
even deeper in the figure, re-placing

peaks to make a Star-in-the-Box! Or, a Diamond-heart-
Star at *every* level (a shape self-similar); a shape
of extreme complication, in only a few—in five—

iterations, it already reads as texture and is rapidly
sinking as it plummets, repeating, into bonded
lock, where photons mediate, shunting between

heavy center, vibrant orbit. Or *deeper,* look. No,
look, a quantum leap: the burst box—the born star—is re-
emerging on the line, on the line *or/and....* Repeat:

Iris an Illusion

Consider
      the ink-charged brush
on Wang Wei's scroll, how the stroke that will mean tree
is nothing like the one for river, though all

is smoke here, barely visible
      plumes and patches: carbon particles of ink
bleeding a border, according to competing capillarities
of fiber in the brush,

the paper. Consider
      the stroke, how it is part of the hill, part
of the middle ground of this scroll from *The White Crane*
series, said to be in Wang Wei's style: repetitions

of direction
      —the roof tiles, say, "echoing" branches;
mountain valleys wrinkled, like rock fissure—
angles of juncture at points on the scroll, not themselves

interlocked there, lock inside
      the rapt observer, who gazes not over
but in and out, now seeing, now not,
an arc in the mist

film will capture,
      though we can't. Call
the rainbow *illusion,* then—
but

gasp
      as that huge fish *in one shimmering*
bound clears the vault, eludes
grasp.

Real Toads

Dreamlike as the garden was, full—filling—as it was
with trysts, wisteria, murmurs to interpret; Heaven-Pattern
of assassins
as it turned out it was, a place with one Namer,
two trees, four speakers sinuously
blaming: *only* dreaming
could have made Him make it, dream solution, Mother-
of-Dream dyeing His brain so deeply green
He moaned and woke—to find it outside Him,
an abrupt project,
landscape: *green-er-y.* Not for that,
less wholly dream; it was dream
to the core,
His garden, His greenness.

In it, badger, smoke, time—orderless creatures. Time,
a creature He tried to annihilate; time,
a badger, big-bellied, awkward, lifting
her head, catching a scent. She backed down
from her branch, slipped her paws in the stream
where His thought flashed in schools, as if scavenging
a minnow, the glint of a pebble, and the stream
grew turbid, its waters went backward
and all they carried, backward, the swill,
the silt: all the dead,
fouling the water, until He repented
even what had come
unbidden, even what He hadn't
dreamed. Still
she stirred.

He repented repenting. He choked in His thought,
in faces of the dead. Livid, rose
from His sleeplessness. To escape these dead
broke into His own dream,
hoping for refuge; found it not the same thing
He adored, waking: the crystallized
green thing. Feared
that difference. Feared
those dead.

To each gate where He'd set a turning angel with cesium sword
and red glass eyes that lit and unlit, He returned
to pull the circuit. Thought again. Went back
again and smashed the angel's
hand, which was a coinbox. Dimes
spurted from the jagged thumb
against the gate, on
the concrete.

In the sudden un-angeled quiet, old sinews, lost tongues, quit gripping
the wall of the cave where they'd hidden; hearing silence
at the entrance, they let go, lengthened. One—or two
whole bodies tumbled from the sky, and crumpled fingers
in loose enough soil pushed up like fescue,
all pale, all stunted. In clumps,
like women or workmen, very few together.
Each, amazed at the surface of the earth, even lying down
and laughing, not too loudly.
The palms held grass blades
to the lips, and the lips whistled—
as if that were enough; as if
what the eyes saw were only
a blindness
eyes are subject
to;

this is what the eyes knew: how close to abortive
such birth was; how time had no way
to parlay a gain, or even repeat it;
how time and the animals were
not allied; how,

already, on the charged horizon,
the odds
had risen too high.

The Romans Captured Archimedes

who was pondering a problem, tracing
circles in his garden. The problem

for them: Archimedes's *Sun
Reflector* firestorming galleys plucked

from Their Sea by his *Claw-
Tongs-On-A-Pulley.* Rome killed

Archimedes, sacked his city: won.
Archimedes, thinking *Levers,*

thought, "If I stood
outside it, I could lift the Earth,"

a goal. Its first, giant, step: mounting
shoulders both ancient and high, Isaac

alone, Isaac
so bitter, Isaac the chronic,

dogged contender, escaping from Plague,
Isaac Newton weighed the sun.

Heaven and Earth, 1666

Copernicus

spoke more or less of the wander
of the earth and Mercury and Mars and the evening star
—which isn't a star—muttering,
"They do, they wander";

Tycho

the Dane kept scrupulous chart of that appearance;

Kepler

from Tycho's tables
drew laws that distressed him—*dung,*
he called them, looking for circles. Wonderful
laws: elongated curves of equal outsweep—elliptical
orbits—their speed increasing closing in on the Sun,
slowing down moving off, always the same
sweeping motion, Mercury, or Mars
or any of the wandering—

then *Newton*

        saw
how it happened, how—Attraction!—their sped-up speed, their onrush
would come if the Sun were pulling on them, figuring
how
        strong a pull that might be, so weighing

          the sun,
and he,
young and the river flowing under him and the apple tree.

TRUE NORTH 2

Our Home the Earth

For help from the spinning earth, you need
a stick driven into the ground.
Turning, earth

makes the Sun appear
to rise and cross the sky—and set in the West.
As the Sun seems to change

position
in the sky, the shadow of the stick
turns and changes

length. When
the shadow is shortest, it points
true

North:
this happens about
noon.

Language Is a Cast of the Human Mind

"Some argue that Gibbs has yet to be fully understood nearly ninety years after his death. With his findings in thermodynamics, and the subsidiary fields of statistical mechanics and vector analysis, however, he singlehandedly laid the foundations for vast portions of modern science, and is now widely regarded as the greatest scientist ever to work at Yale, and the foremost American scientist of all times."

"Sixteen of the world's leaders in mathematical physics, physical chemistry, astrophysics, mathematics, geology, biology, and economics, including three Nobel Prize winners, [spoke] about the ways in which their own work follows from that of [this] nineteenth-century scientist . . . [whose] work was so advanced that one of his great admirers, Albert Einstein, complained about one of his papers that 'it is hard to read and the main points have to be read between the lines.'"

—Marc Wortman, "A Loner's Legacy," 1989

American Speech

Resistance to tyrants *is* obedience to God.
        Don't Tread On Me!
                The Connecticut Valley

has to be
        the most
                abstract location in the universe—minds

of winter, minds of Iceland spar, at work
        in Dickinson, Edwards,
                Peirce,

and Gibbs. The whole a hotbed
        of revival, of Great Awakening: the one
                word

Noah Webster invented, of all those
        in his book,
                demoralise,

a slow
        seep into melting snow and gray afternoon;
                Gibby, skating

long strokes on the pond; Emily
        watching freedom
                condense

inside the clear glass of her window.
        In this Valley, neighbors
                disregard

—sustain—hidden fervence, run Underground
        railroads; *Images and Shadows*
                sewn up

in Edwards's notebooks, flint
    stitched into Dickinson's, 700
        equations

of Gibbs's great paper set up in type at last
    by shopkeepers'
        subscription: in CT, they

Make Do, but they tore
    the house, the home on High Street, Gibbs's—born
        and died there—down.

Young Willard Gibbs Is a Physicist

at home, in the home at High and Wall
he never left, his emotional life
"not fought for," Muriel said—

Rukeyser, who fought for his biography.
Self-appointed. Against her, cohorts
of colleagues and family who like Dickinson

kinsmen "Suffocate — with easy woe — "
all trace, all access to. Gibbs wasn't frail,
but strong. Not shy, presiding. At home

with ideas; not, with people—yet, if it were
important, he would praise: eulogizing
Clausius; if it were *very* important,

he would fight: over vectors, with Tait.
". . . but I believe that there is a deeper
question of notions underlying

that of notations. Indeed, if my offence
had been solely in the matter
of notation. . . ."

Maxwell said: There is no more powerful way
to introduce knowledge to the mind than . . . as many different
ways as we can, wrenching the mind

away
from the symbols to the objects and from the objects
back to the symbols.

Maxwell said: I have been striving all my life to be free
of the yoke of Cartesian co-ordinates. I found
such an instrument in

quaternions. Do I need *quaternions*
to talk about light?
Alas,

the square of quaternions
is negative. But Gibbs's vectors, uncouth
seemingly, work

well, in *any* dimension, with a very
great capability for
interpreting space relations.

Rukeyser said: Critical minds
that approach the world with love
have but one possible

defense—to build a system.
Rayleigh said, I protest
the compression.

Gibbs: I myself concluded
that the paper was
too long.

From Plain to Pure

So
to frame observation
as to make God speak: science creates

alert, disciplined—regenerate—perception. Absolute
validity
of the sensuous

> in CT: *We could never have conceived of these,*
> *if we had not seen them; and now, we can think of nothing*
> *beyond them,*

Edwards said. The obliquity
of love does not in fact disable it. Frank celebration
being

> denied, direct apprehension: the Truth set out
> before him, naked, leaning through a veil
> of shifting snow, awaits

elucidation. Have we moved no
farther, then—than
from ingenuity to insight, private judgment with a vengeance?

Men hate
to die, Edwards said, *because they cannot bear*
to let go of the beauty of the world,

> but Dickinson
> said,
> *I guard My Master's Head —*

"It Is You Talking Just as Much

as myself—I act as the tongue
> of you," he said, or wrote: Walt Whitman. *Who?* Who *is*
>> this massing, polled, this multi-point self?

"I showed her Heights she never saw —
> And now — 'Woulds't have me for a Guest?'
>> She could not find her Yes —"

Dickinson wrote. Then
> re-wrote, *as*
>> "He showed me heights I never saw —"

Deeper
> duplicity: none. Role, trope, and object: all
>> reversing, as if all were one

affair—
> of language.
>> Cooing,

the bird outside my window takes no notice,
> mid-morning or dawn or supper, it is mournful: *Oh but—who-*
> *who-who* the form of its floating

sorrow, so intent
> and equable now in its sorrow, so patient
>> and outbreathing

now, of its sorrow. I had
> hoped to find the iris tended
>> still, in Gibbs's garden; I thought women

of that town, if they had
> a garden club, or League, would come with dark blue
>> bulbs

or yellow-tongued; I thought they would keep
    a Garden, but
        they tore it

limb from limb, beheading, dripping, tore the house
    on High
        Street down.

Jus Suum: *What Can Never Be Taken*

JOSIAH WILLARD GIBBS, 1790–1861

... that the *question*
can be tolerated—whether they be

freemen—for
a single moment, Gibbs said

(Josiah Willard, the Elder, Professor at Yale
of sacred books). *Language*

is a cast of the human mind
Gibbs Elder said, visiting the jail

in 1839, to give theirs back
to them, on "our" soil: transcribing

sounds, for words
for numbers, told to him

from behind their bars
when he held up his fingers: 1, 2, . . . 5, . . . 10;

then traveling to New York, by stagecoach,
ship, to the port, to seek—and find,

on a British brig, someone who spoke
Mendi *and* English,

that African men, Black mutineers,
might claim their right—should they

have had to? Inalienable—
in an American court,

convened in Connecticut, *New Haven,*
where the slaveship was tied up.

Our courts,
he said. The shame

to our courts, that the question could be tolerated
(whether

they be freemen—regaining their freedom—
or criminals, or property)

for a single

moment.

EMILY ELIZABETH DICKINSON, 1830–1886
JOSIAH WILLARD GIBBS, 1839–1903

Never married, never moved from their Family Home.

> *I am so potent, I can reach you only after wave upon wave*
> *of dilution. You will re-discover, but not read me.*
> *I have built a language to make my work more pure.*

A pure inquiry—into unity—has concerned this nation
ever since it claimed Independence through union. Cornerstones
of the Church on the Green in New Haven, monuments

to Regicide: Dickinson, a Fire Bride, a bomb, a volcano. As alive,
or more so, in the grave as out of it. Showing us this across the garden
fence of the grave. Speaking in the tomb, of the tomb, as of a ride,

one of many, every poem one of many, No-name inquiries—
but we have her numbered. *Is* Dickinson articulate? Did Higginson,
Johnson, Franklin—would Bloom, if Bloom spoke of her—make her

articulate? She said the grave gave her language.
Whitman said the future, always sampling the future, enlisting the future,
and Gibbs a prisoner, of his own unwillingness to auction

his mind, who built a mathematic language to make his work *more pure*—
who made it so pure, it sublimed instantly into zones of power
and remains enthroned there, isolated there. The supremely

articulate among us, *Amistad* Africans, mutineers for freedom
on the ship they commandeered, stole from the captain and steered
by their own light—and by starlight—to a New World, a rock-bound

coast; a world not wilderness alone, but Wilderness with courts
in it, and canon, and codes of presentation, a world of sacred
language their own language attacked, active virus, ancient

knowledge that it was, *they* perplex— No translator.
No way-maker. No wizard wise woman sponsor. Only the Valley
itself of the Connecticut River, who brought from itself,

with the help of Sarah, Jonathan Edwards. A valley
itself with its snow and snow water. So far from Home.

> *I am so potent, I can reach you only by submitting*
> *to wave upon wave of dilution. So potent*
> *only I can reach you: now. Soon.*

Prometheus, or The Eagle's Prey

Coming
to understand that slavery is

not less widespread
in the modern world than in the ancient, that slavery

lasts, that war
endures—afflictions that

from the outside seem easy to bear,
normal

to go on, last, endure,
of their own weight: they rob,

they devour
the resource required to throw them off: inner

life. And any rise
of life, at first, in any slave,

appears as love
of its owner: fabling

a relation, not to sense so
directly the repeated crushing

power; to aver,
to dissemble

a need to hide that overcomes
the afflicted,

for they are dressed: bound
and exhibited

in their degradation—Prometheus
nailed, in the open, on

the rock. Prey to all.
Parched by light.

Gibbs making found

what lies hidden, so deeply nested
is it within, so down
deeply pocketed, miles

from the icy, calm, notational
surface: making a line,
a lure, one symbol, one elliptical

expression, holding echo
upon echo, decoding
to a catalog: an infinite

acceptance . . .

detonation

as almost welcome and always
implicit
in the mind, like the cloud, low,
and going to snow

in CT. Great still pool. Demoralized
desire that waits for
snow
as if the snow were

winged

Even Purits Forced to Re-Cog

1

Even Purits forced to re-cog that *HB*
was so purely imagic, that maximany *KJ* version
metaps decode overly varigatal

meanings, manysome not in *Westminst.*
Confessio. O. My. Outsiderlaw *Confessio.*
From the beginning, Purits employ

tech-lore as rhetor bells. Honest
Jonny Edwards: modern religion! O
My. One great reason why

speculative points are thought to be of so
little importance. O. My. Consists so little
in respect to. "We have so far

lost respect for God that we are openly permitting
. . . ingenuity. The Sun. . . ." Purits want no
diversion, no Anglican polity, no sweet

sermon, no diversion of attention
from thematic
assertion: sinner Perdicamen.

2

Honest Jonny Edwards, Yale 1720,
reading Isaac Newton, *Principia*, Cambridge,
1687: equall claims to authority,

Thesis, Thing, Event. Old rhetoric goes,
Jon says, if, as *is* so, old physics dead.
His secret, sustained effort to be rid

of the old: to make way for the older,
old as Origen; his effort to recover, by New
Science, to see as if None had seen, Gibbs

or Dickinson, but the first in that Valley
was Jonathan. No longer to illustrate
the meaning of what's said,

but the Truth of what is: Exempla
—not emblems. Their own
selves. Standing for themselves.

3

In CT, waves of wet snow, in waves
of gravitation. Receiving the vision,
Mathema-physics, Locke's psychology,

the Universe Organized around
an act of mind: the knowable confined
to the reach of lengthening instrumentation

and the mind's self-knowing and their inter-
penetration. If God had left off speaking,
once code was stated, briefly,

then Rhetoric should too. The tangible
world intaken: intelligible. The fact
of experience, a shadow of God: the act

of cognition a moment of fusion in which
a thing finds its concept—and is found.
This is a mind of snow in Connecticut.

This is a Snow Mind knowing as if None
knew. Exhilarated. Brilliant. An eagle
at the breast of the whitening world.

Holding the Other Hostage

How the opposed breed each other: cast
and mold, they *are* one boundary: all

inversions re-inforce, for between them
they rule: they rule out. They cleave

together, and better than love, are
righteously cruel: white Slave-

holding Mistress. Their epithets mean
you are strangely polluted, you

immigrant Alien, Jew, Gentile
dog. How to change their success? Change

the neighborhood. Change what you call
"dark"; I, "intimate." Control means to hold

the *contre-rôle*, the duplicate register.
What of the night? Who knits there?

Real Life Is White in Connecticut

pale green
and white in Connecticut trees elms The Common
the sky the mind in Connecticut calcite bar
of burning crystal prism on the sill

      iris in the garden
      charts and charters
      sea-bitten shore

permitting oneself little that little cold
sharp as bramblepoints in air seeded with new snow
to come in Connecticut outpouring down pouring
crystals to come full of the hint and intimation
of snow the overwhelming darkening white of the snow
burying bodies in CT blinding angled sheet of its softness
biting at the shore of the sky

iris—itself—short sword in the pale
green spring of CT unassuming
terse

      April snow
      stained by flowers

It's Hard

The noontime shadow changes length very slowly.
The noontime shadow is only *one* length: its length at noon.
The noontime shadow—my watch

is usually off, anyway. It's hard—I mean, it's difficult
what with the little ridges in the dust,
the cellophane-silvery

glare on the sand, trying to track it over
those few moments. It was getting shorter: that much was clear,
that part was easy. And then,

it dawns
on you, or dusks, getting longer
again, yes, indubitably;

but that zone, that zero, that anxiety
of getting it just, so, at its very
consensual

shortest: things are changing
now, here, so minutely, with such delicacy, North,
and noon, and this sort

of wonderful
vertical
stick.

Numbers Nesting in Numbers-
Nesting-In Numbers

0

Nothing that is not there and the nothing that is.
—Wallace Stevens, "The Snow Man"

Out the door *every*
day along High Street
to Sloane. Only the grave
there still and the grave gates, Egyptian,
red soft sandstone. Every
day. Truth not flowing down
from a source; but, an exact
accord that makes the whole
simpler than the parts;
those bodies lost all winter
in the snow. The storm
in the night so great,
so erasing the man

so immemorably standing in it, at sea in it,
and the woman in batiste weeds of white at sea
in it on her widowed watching walk.

Gibbs spoke only once
in a Faculty Meeting, during
protracted, tiring debate on elective courses:
should there be—more English, more Classics? More? Or less.
They were astonished to see him rise, after thirty-two years,
though familiar with the high, pained-sounding voice: a man of snow
assessing. Not to be distracted, or dispersed into longcuts,
not to be turned from the whole entire empty mist
hanging in the cold air, not to miss—or
intrude on the nothing that was
there.

Escaping
in every emotional way,
Gibbs, hidden at home, creating the loneliness
he needed to assume just one responsibility—for which no thanks,
much complaining of it, some wonder. Lost, in the clouds of snow gathering

in CT over *Transactions & Proceedings* of the local Academy of Sciences,
the one un-evasion he accepted: shortcutting elegance by uncouth
statement that is efficient in every respect. The reward for
getting past the failings of language? To be found
un-readable. Gibbs rose. He said: *Mathematics
is a language.* And sat down.

1 *Natural Numbers*

( )

Attending to Red,
        to 1 as it turns and turns

into *Unio(n)*, the child
                    who hunts
is the child who herds,

        riveted

at night
                by stars

in the heat,
        as she sleeps

    in the mint-

    mild

yard.

(( )

The Silver Power
of Zero makes a mirror-

realm: *Are-not.*
Domain

trails from itself the ink
Minus, sign of Debt,

of Doubt, of Double-
entry: books to keep

or doubled sets
of points to win. *Zero-*

sum? Of two,
one wins. Only one.

$$((\,(\,)\,))$$

A ratio(n) game: a game for three. A game?
Or resonant arc. Fi(r)st catch the snake, defang and milk
its poison teeth. Pocket

it. Then eat—as if eating poppy seed—your poppy seeds.
Would you like some of my seed?
say to the girl. *O, I'm*

sorry,
but my hands are dirty. Just reach in
to my . . . pocket

(me). Who carries this
off, this locket-transparent transfer/collapse of structure,
deceit, and the natural world, this child's

play, this Blueprint inscribed with white
numbers—the Plan, with all, indicated,
gaps—enters it, adult.

(((( ))))

The need to write down numbers: not some, but All,

and I can do it—and I do, euphoric, disquiet—All is smaller
than few by far by Far, a series summed, a limit
passed-to and subsumed, itself now item;

a method: for Truth, which means here

depth, the Peirce-ing range, the finer mesh, the even deeper
reach through layer into layer holding
up: still true, still *truer*. Not logical, not only;

the truth of a ravening child who must find

divinity Exact—exactly to find it: Pythagoras stopped
and offered sacrifice to God when he discovered
that the circle was

a locus of means. Far-seer. Canny conceiver. With a snake

in his pocket, but ravenous, retreating from few
to All, to four corners of the wind, of the world
turning gold, gold as corn and pumpkin. Gold as control.

(IM   (RE   (RA   (IN   (NA   ))))

I spell it out—
          to spell it in; I cast a spell
    that puts an end
to all distinction: more including, wider flung, closer spun, more pen-
etrant, or more in-
    fusing, if we only knew what
empty space *was*—the solid part of a table *one* part in each Quadrillion:
    Im Re.Rainna: Im Re.writing the Imaginary
Natural Integral Rational Real

      as

Identical. Crimson. 5. Uprising droplet petals
    resist
        disappearance, de-
vitrify: star at the skin
and grow
inward in the form
of
    Iota:

      Iota
      and her anti-self
      cancel: Iota,
      dividing herself, is still
      hidden: none,
      but one; but Iota,[+]
      returned to herself, overlaying
      herself, an enfolding
      Revelation
      of One who-is-and-is-not-one, who is Not-one, who
      returned
      to herself is real, and Minus: rotational

[+] $\sqrt{-1}$

Spine
—Girder and
Axis
of description in the
(actual) quantum
mechanical
world, in the
Body
Electric.

Strategem Strategem

You can measure more easily
when the shadow length changes more rapidly: morning,
afternoon. Take a rope.
Tying yourself

to your fixed stick—don't bend it—and pulling
the rope
taut, walk a circle: you
are the point

now,
of your own compass. Once
in the morning, once in the afternoon, the tip
of the stick's shadow

will touch
on your circle, and where it does
must become for you
new centers:

staking these—new stakes, old rope—
inscribe arcs
in the sand, walking them off, first one,
then the other. The arc

of the morning
and the arc of the afternoon
will cross. Between your
stick

and this crossover
point lies the line leading
North:
about Noon,

the seemingly
moving Sun will draw it—
with a shadow
mark.

There Was an Old Woman

"Cailleac Beara. A famous hag of Irish and Scottish folklore. Her name is reported as Dirri or Digdi . . . sometimes also called the Old Woman of Dingle. She is called the Hag of Beare because she had fifty foster children on the Island of Beare off the west coast of Ireland in Bantry Bay."

"Her many lovers, her great age, and her renewal of youth are the features of her story."

"The word itself, *cailleac,* means veiled woman and lends itself to the double interpretation of hooded hag or veiled nun. . . . Probably she is best known today because of the beautiful poem, *The Lament of the Old Woman of Beare* . . . out of a 10th century manuscript. . . ."

"Many a huge rock is her bed or chair; many a cairn is her grave. . . . The Hebrides were formed from loose rocks which fell from her apron. . . . The Whirlpool of the Corry-vrecken between Jura and Scorva is also attributed to her; the one spot especially where the waters 'boil up white' is called the Cailleac."

    —Funk & Wagnalls, *Standard Dictionary of Folklore*

Above the Steeple, or Vector Victorious

    1 Spinning

The Iron Angel standing in the North, reaching nothing as
she turns on the field of the winds, deranged
by her turning, waylaid, worn—*is*

turned, spun, flung hard back: an Iron Rod she cannot
break? An iron rod, she does not
bend:

in the maelstrom, outswirling
vortex; held to rigid
stillness when

prevailing
power comes for her, drawn
by the sail of her hair, her wing, the longstem of her horn—

2 On Guard

She is her post, she is the wanton wind:
she is the driven snow—and she is drive;
but she is not that tiny water drop

plummeting through tides of swooping cold
to form an ice-rinsed knob, a feathered branch,
a burst of radiant, hexagonic jewels

that float as skeins of frost, as hoar that clings
to rippled iron of her hair, to frozen grooves
inside her wing; a counterpane

blankets softly, now, twig, lantern, withered
bush; slowing, sifting heaviness: a bed,
dim, moon-silvered, where the children take

brightness for their dream from moonbeams cast
through gauze, through tangled birchbroom tapping
branches at their glass, dangling down

to scatter glistening whorls across the ground
and shatter, spun like spoons against that wall
where fisted pillows settle under heads

themselves aweigh, piping in the clouds
and throwing buckets over, giving chase
to leaping galaxies of foam, now

blinding the still air above the pond,
above the schoolyard swing, the silver-domed
Observatory downhill from the Church,

garden paths edged with cockle shells,
filling dogwood forks, the stiffened shrub
that will not bud again, new graves, old stones,

a sled left out, and lifting, now, to swirl
the bells blown through the darkened arch,
now looping inward, upward, tongueing bells.

1. Newbery published *The History of Little Goody Two Shoes*, generally ascribed to Goldsmith, in 1765.

2. According to Dr. Sam Johnson, Goldsmith also sang it on the night of January 29, 1768, to console himself on the poorly received opening of his play, *The Good Natur'd Man*.

3. A strange way of putting it.

4. Interestingly enough, Thomas had married a granddaughter of Thomas and Elizabeth Fleet, and so was related, on the distaff side, to old "Mother Goose" herself.

5. Later versions would have you believe that the old woman was tossed in a "basket."

6. In later versions, the poor old dear is tossed "ten," "nineteen," "fifty," "seventy," even "ninety-nine" times as high as the moon. We'll settle for seventeen—a mere 4,060,570 miles.

7. The earliest printed version of this song available to us today appears (just as it is given here) in the Preface to Newbery's *Melody*. The Preface writer says:
"When [Henry V of England] turned his arms against France, he composed a march to lead his troops to battle, well knowing that music has often the power of inspiring courage, especially in the minds of good men. Of this his enemies took advantage, and, as our happy nation, even at that time, was never without a faction, some of the malcontents adopted words [of the rhyme] to the king's own march, in order to ridicule his majesty, and to show the folly and impossibility of his undertaking . . . . Here the king is represented as an old woman, engaged in a pursuit the most absurd and extravagant imaginable; but when he had routed the whole French army at the battle of Agincourt, taking their king and the flower of the nobility prisoners, and with ten thousand men only made himself master of their kingdom; the very men who had ridiculed him before, began to think nothing was too arduous for him to surmount, they therefore cancelled the former sonnet, which they were now ashamed of, and substituted this in its stead, which you will please to observe goes to the [same tune as the king's march]."
"So vast is the prowess of Harry the Great,
He'd pluck a hair from the pale fac'd moon;

Historical, Philosophical and Critical" which embellish the little volume.

"Mother Goose" rhymes—"the most celebrated Songs and Lullabies of the good old Nurses, calculated to amuse Children and to excite them to sleep"[3] make up the first part of the *Melody*. There are fifty-two of them in all, but a large number of these had been printed earlier, and we have already encountered them; some we shall meet later.

The second part of the *Melody* contains songs "of that sweet Songster and Nurse of Wit and Humour, Master William Shakespeare"—a fact that some scholars think gives color to the impression that Shakespeare was among the wits who secretly penned a number of the rhymes that may possibly be political pasquinades.

No copy of the first edition of the *Melody* is known to exist, but the volume was reprinted, in 1786, by Isaiah Thomas of Worcester, Mass., and sold at his bookstore in that city.[4] No complete copy of this 1786 printing has been found, to date. The earliest known perfect copy, one of a printing made in 1794, is in the library of the American Antiquarian Society at Worcester. From this copy, William H. Whitmore (in 1889), W. F. Prideaux (in 1904), and Frederick G. Melcher (in 1945) produced facsimile editions, Whitmore's with a long and scholarly historical introduction.

Here, now, are the rhymes added by Newbery and Goldsmith to the rising tide of "Mother Goose" melodies.

« 35 »

There was an old woman toss'd in a blanket,[5]
Seventeen times as high as the moon;[6]
But where she was going no mortal could tell,
For under her arm she carried a broom.
Old woman, old woman, old woman, said I!
Whither, ah whither, ah whither so high?
To sweep the cobwebs from the sky,
And I'll be with you by and by.[7]

Hag of Beare, or the Calendar Girl

1

Of Gaimar's *Lestorie* . . . , Book 2 alone
remains to us, stories and strains
of the English, the Anglo "Sack-sons"
who burn down the woods and who gain
on the lost ones, the ones of Book 1
—old Britain's old book at Ox(en)ford
lost, with old Bretons: the pain
of beginning again at Book 2, when
Book 1, when book won, when Book One. . . .

A marching song! Do you believe
what they say, that some malcontents
adapted King Harry's own march
to ridicule His war pursuits
at Agincourt? *Mad arrogance*
to pit but these few at these many,
did they say? Did they sing, but to taunt,
old Harry, old woman, old folly?
Or is there another account to account

for a reckoning prayer so old— Not 1765,
but 17,000 years ago, when ibex belled
on the glacial hill and salmon fought
upstream, when bilberries bloomed
under frozen oak, and the women, together,
bled, how *did* a community die?
By ice. By losing track. Of how
far they are from the Sun, just how many
days to trek back . . . they slowly forget

where winter *is,* lose their way to calibrate
a calendrical Year—of the Sun—
with the Horn of women's Blood
as it measures: ten moons to a birth;
so lose all way to anticipate that slow
drift—for the Star-Web shifts, as
they move through their hunting grounds,
as they move through years of their life;
lose, then, all way to predict

the deeper drift for them, their sons'
and daughters' sons, who will wander in a mindless
maze of bilberries, blood, and snow—unless
some child while watching the sky re-sees
Three Graces whose tripling, turning, tilt
she saw *before* on walls of the cave, flying
above her by flickering torch, three views in time
of spinning form, and deciphers in full
from tangling lines a body, a Pear in foliage,

the body of earth, earth's body, whole, Blue
Planet inscribed on earth's core to say: Go,
there, my child, where the Arctic Bear
is speared, where the Seated Woman stays,
where Draco the Dragon Eel swims and plays
in foam at her feet in the sky, and know
the circles are circling
themselves. Even the Poles
are an ebb and a flow, their circling stems

mark a hole in the sky, locked
to the stroke of a butterfly's wing, locked
to a wave in the heart of a stone on the farthest
star you can't see, but going ahead

to your home, the woman in *Harry's* song
—as they *tell* us. Peace, she is saved,
by whatever means come to hand, for you
to ponder, to graze, in your heart, to swing
on the horns of your hurtful mind:

There was an old woman tossed up in a basket,
Seventeen times as high as the moon;

But where she was going no mortal could tell
For under her arm she carried a broom.

Old woman, old woman, old woman, quoth I!
Whither, ah whither, ah whither so high?

To sweep the cobwebs from the sky,
And I'll be with you by and by.

2

As Ancient forests, turned to black blood
by the weight of the earth, are put alight

by the rocket's glare, by the Brilliant Bombs
bursting red in the bitter air, a Cockpit womb

exploding there, the Challenger
in fiery flight, the Hag of Beare

burning in air, the sea itself set afire by night
will turn on the earth, will hold its waves

coherent, drone one wailing dirge—one gathering might
will surge away from the vortices, the hissing cry

of little wheels and one wall rise, one shrug, one massing
watery wall—no breaking fall, no broken power,

no canceling phase, but racing its way
and gaining speed in straits at the Drake

for towering miles: implacable tons, of frozen
hollow watery boom erase green earth, dislodge the moon

from fragile orbit: flame and slag the meteoric
womb of moon come hurtling down—

the flying broom a woman rode, a woman alone
at her sweeping work, saving leavings,

accounted prayer, reckoning remnant patch
and scrap, leastings, faintly floating webs

of star-drift, woman aligned with a Goose,
astride the Mother who navigates, who flies

in formation though skies are falling,
who flies though the Poles themselves

aren't fixed—what Cup, what Broom,
what Web, what Term? Over

the rainbow? Open
sky? A moveable home—to none

denied? With you. With you.
By—and by.

Who,

then, sweeps
them loose, who diffuses

broken, shining bits, the farflung force
washed to foam on a rockface, succulents

and whelks alive inside
its razing spray? Who slings

the broth aslide in cups of ocean swell? Whose bolt
of lace, a great spill of it blowing

in the window with her pins, patterns the firmament, patterns
the phosphorescent body of an Eel making slip-knots

in the dark sea, patterns fireflies sailing
through grass at the edge

of a wood, lit—and unlit—at twilight, giving
body to the air,

or to some, brimming, being
—whose? Who?

Narrowness of Narrow Path Endured

Identical in nature, but differing
in phase, are we at odds? Can we be contained
on a riling, ruthlessly captained, single ship?

It swirls like a stick in the whirlpool at the Straits.

Can we be controlled by a motherly gaze? By the tottering
walk of a mother-to-be who caresses the already-born
with eyes and tongue, but self-absorbed

in the one-to-come, sways as she walks catching the sun

on one shoulder, then another, perambulating mother?
Or by him, one of the roughs, melding
with the crowd—with them all, but untouched?

Can we be compassed by thought? "Let us imagine,"

said Gibbs, abstracting pure Rule,[+] that will fuel
the Third Reich, "a great number of independent
systems. . . ." Most certainly at odds. Most certainly competing.

Can they be assessed? In a lab? At a desk? Can they

be changed? By a go-between? With their disastrous
capability of relaxing the entire, the major, the inherent
interconnection of this extended system back . . . to

snow, to fall-out in the dark, to frozen

[+] The Phase Rule, a description of equilibrium based on a new way of conceiving
this state—in terms of "degrees of freedom."

rock surrounded by black pine, back-lit by the enormity of
no-longer-starlight illumining the dance
of a ghostly dancer—highwayman

in the snow, who longing to see her dance, exposed,

waylays, waylaid her. O little girls, with your babble
and braids, putting raincoats on the babies, talking
the toddlers out of fright

at the lightning, one of you shinnying the radiator pole—

one, with bursting cheeks; you older girls, not allowing
cursing on the landing, where all seek shelter
from the sudden summer storm: not

yet the prolonged voluptuous seen—and reseen—reseen

rescene: immolating stormflight of the young motherteacher
burned again and again before the eyes of her daughter
and her son; not narrow enough, the path of control,

Canaveral, Chernobyl— Not narrow, at all.

TRUE NORTH 5

It's Easy

at the South Pole. There *every*
direction
is true North. Direction, there, itself

the point
turning and moving,
or the place

where you look, if you still
stand waiting.
Though

you forget
all the steps—forget!
Remember,

every,
and so *easy,*
at

the nadir.

To Be Here as Stone Is

Gloss of green on a stone— Cold waterfall, a ripple
down the uneven globe of this tiny amphora, this ampoule
for perfume scored by a comb in the molten
bottle: fountain strands
of sea-green jade and sea-light opal in sheaths of fire
remelt, re-fuse to new luster in which bubbles
shift and drops of vapor, sealed in glaze, at each angle catch light—
catch *light!* That *cry*—annihilation made, outbound forever till
it hits your eye and ends, a green glow, all
you see, extinguished starlight, starlight only. Focused
by stone, cleaved, bruted, brilliant-cut. No stone like that
exists, before 1600. No world—until us—in chains of glass, hostage
to signal: all clearness & purity, fidelity,
integrity, traits of the channel, its internal reflection. Objects
are answers, unspoken collusions of humans with the earth
as it turns, as it culminates in night-skies on Neptune, Earth
as it sweeps by, or is swept—it depends where you are—
by schools of light, loose, adrift in the empty
aisles of the cosmos: this, their care
—the artisans—their persistent reverence for error,
mis-fit; fabulists of silica, water, what we are,
glassware, charcoal, starlight only; forgers of green,
translucent stones that are the structure of all question.